because crack is Illegal

a 30-day devotional for moms

by raema mauriello

table of contents:

I have had a lot of experiences in life, but nothing comes close to being a mother. It has changed my life and it's been an experience unlike any other. I served in the Navy as a Journalist and as a Search and Rescue Swimmer, I've been married for 12 years, been a stay at home mom for 7 years, been in full time ministry for 9 years (doing everything from leading the children's ministry, helping to plant a church to speaking on a platform), I enrolled as a full time college student just 2 months before my fourth child was born, and I've also been a room mom at my boys' school.

It is definitely rewarding but it is not glamorous... at all. Kids cry, they smell, they say inappropriate things at inappropriate times, they leave a mess, they eat off of the floor, they pick their noses, they fight with each other, they like to hide in clothes racks at the store (which triggers a reaction in us that sounds something like a Velociraptor as we scream their names), they like to run away from us in parking lots, they draw a lot of unrequested comments from strangers in public, and did I mention they cry?

Through this journey I have had high highs and low lows and none of my children are teenagers yet. I struggled with depression after having children, so I know the feeling of helplessness and purposelessness that we can sometimes feel. I know what it's like to not shower for days. I know what it's like to drop your kids off at school in your pajamas. I know what it's like to hide in a closet so you can eat candy without getting asked for a bite. I know what it's like to dream about going to bathroom without interruption. I know what it's like to live on coffee. I know that a frequent question running through our minds is, "will my kids need therapy?" I know what it's like to laugh when your child dumps clear nail polish on your couch because that's all you can do at that point. Being a mom is ridiculous sometimes, so I wanted to write a 30-day devotional just for you! To make you laugh; to remind you that it's going to be ok, that you are not alone, and that this too shall pass.

This book is for you, mom who spends endless moments in a carline, who barely slept last night, who isn't sure what she is doing or if what she is doing is right, who works outside of the home then comes home and works some more, who is holding it down without support, who has dreams in her heart that seem too far off, who picks boogers out of her kids' noses then wipes it on her pants, who hasn't eaten a warm meal in years, who waits to go inside the house because your child fell asleep in the car, who compares her parenting to parents on social media, who is convinced they have lost their salvation, who just needs some chocolate and a nap! Whatever stage your kids are in, I dedicate this book to you.

Grab a Bible and a journal to capture the things God wants to speak to you as you walk through these next 30-days.

From my family...to yours!

Raema Mauriello

(From left to right: Dominic, Brayden, Jordan, Gabby, Raema, and Asher)

3

As I am looking at a jacket in the women's department I turn around and to my horror Asher is holding a bra and says, "Mom, do you like this shirt? You could get this one." Then to follow that up Brayden is holding women's underwear and says, "how about some of these butt pants....you could get these ones."

God is still good

Life has a funny way of throwing the unexpected at you. You're going through life feeling like you have it all together and then BAM! Your two boys are holding up women's underwear in a store and you are rendered completely speechless. I'm not speechless very often, but when I am it's a pretty profound moment in my life. This life we live can throw things our way that are not expected, but how we handle the unexpected is what really matters.

In January of 2014 I woke up in a puddle of blood. Knowing that this was not normal I called my doctor in a panic and they brought me in immediately for an ultrasound to see what was happening. My husband, Jordan, and I sat there in silence as the tech took pictures. In the past every ultrasound I had was while I was pregnant, but this time the monitor was not facing me and the tech wasn't making cute statements about a baby. Her face was serious and I knew something wasn't right. Normally in moments like these I would try to make light of the circumstances and bring laughter into a tense situation...but this time I had nothing funny to say. I was rendered speechless. We were moved into a room for what seemed like an eternity to wait for the doctor, but finally a doctor who wasn't my normal doctor came in. She was holding the ultrasound pictures and her expression was serious. She said, "You have a growth on your left ovary that is the size of a grapefruit. Your doctor is in surgery and we are trying to get him over here to talk with you." Then she left the room.

I would say that I am a pretty strong person. I can usually see the positive in hard situations, but in this moment I couldn't look at Jordan because I knew I would lose it, and I hate crying. All kinds of thoughts started to rush through my brain: Was it cancer? What was it? Who is going to take care of my kids? Jordan can't really cook; everyone is going to starve to death! And what happens if he gets remarried? I would have to come back from the dead and kill people. What will everybody do without ME??? Listen, it was not one of my finest hours.

A day later I had another appointment with my doctor and he reassured me that it was most likely just a benign tumor but we needed to have it removed right away. I am a pretty healthy person. I rarely get sick (because quite frankly I don't have time to get sick), I don't get injured, and I have never had to have surgery. This was all new territory for me. Apparently my ovaries did not get the memo that I did not give them permission to grow extra things and that I don't have time for their crap!

In this moment I had a choice. Either I believe that God is still good, even now, or not. We prayed that God would heal me and that the growth would disappear, but that is not how he chose to heal me. Even still, He is in control. It says in Psalm 136:1, *"Give thanks to the LORD, for he is good. His love endures forever."* This is what I chose to believe, and this is what I will continue to believe. It doesn't say anywhere that this life is going to be easy, but it says our God is good. When we choose to say this in the midst of the hard times, it takes the sting out of the situation. This took my focus off of the enormity of what lay before me and placed it at the feet of God, and His enormity trumped the situation, hands down.

When things happen in our lives that we never see coming we get to make the choice to praise Him anyway. He is the keeper of our lives and we need to remember that He sees all and knows all. Even when all hell breaks loose, He is good. Today, even if you are in the midst of a storm, choose to say, "I trust you" and "God, you are good." This frame of thought removes the pressure from us to try and figure it out, and puts the situation into God's hands. His hands are the only ones I trust to make the wrong things right. He has never let us down and He isn't going to start now.

for reflection:

- What situation are you in where you need to make the choice to believe that God is good? Is it a sickness or a loss? Is it a disappointment?
- How can you place your focus on God and not the current circumstances?

"Asher, stop singing and put your clothes on!"

worth in a **plastic bag**

I'm not sure what it is about being naked that seems so right to kids. I'm also not sure at what point we start to HATE being naked and want to put as many layers of clothing on as possible. Nobody wants to be exposed and put in a position to be completely vulnerable. That's a very intimidating thought.

The day came when I went in for surgery. We filled out the paperwork and a nurse brought Jordan and me back to a room where they would prep me for surgery. I was told to take off all my clothes. I wasn't allowed to wear make-up or lotion (Who wants to have dry skin when you are going to be NAKED in front of strangers? If I have to be naked I would at least like to be moisturized!). I had to take off my wedding ring and place all my belongings in a plastic bag. Everything that was mine was now in a plastic bag. Everything that I identified myself with was removed. Isn't that funny? Everything that I found worth in could fit into a bag? I was doing ok emotionally because Jordan was still in the room with me being my rock, but when he was escorted away I was left in that room alone. Un-moisturized and in a very attractive hospital gown.

As I laid there on a table being pumped with drugs, before I fell asleep, I was thinking about how I found a lot of my worth in titles and things and how ridiculous that all seemed in that moment. Then I heard, "You are mine" and I felt God's overwhelming peace as I fell asleep.

We are HIS. That is the only thing we need to identify ourselves by. It's so easy to get carried away with covering ourselves up with the things of this world. With wearing the things that we have as a part of our identity. I held so tightly to the titles of: mother, wife, pastor, graduate, leader, speaker, mentor, friend. I allowed these things to give me value and worth, but when I was lying on a surgery table all I had left was the fact that I was His, and that is all that mattered.

You are HIS. All of these titles and other things that we have and hold onto are honestly temporary, but the thing that will remain constant is that you belong to Him. Colossians 3:9-11 in the Message Bible says, *"Don't lie to one another. You're done with that old life. It's like a filthy set of ill-fitting clothes you've stripped off and put in the fire. Now you're dressed in a new wardrobe. Every item of your new way of life is custom-made by the Creator, with his label on it. All the old fashions are now obsolete. Words like Jewish and non-Jewish, religious and irreligious, insider and outsider, uncivilized and uncouth, slave and free, mean nothing. From now on everyone is defined by Christ, everyone is included in Christ."* I want to constantly remind myself of this truth. Not even the labels that I have from my past like unwed mother, adulterer, abuser, impure, alcoholic, have a hold on me; and your past doesn't define who you are either! These labels don't own me anymore and they aren't who I am. I am His. We are HIS with HIS label on us.

Honestly anything could have happened on that table in the hospital, and if it had been my time to go, well…His love is so much better than this life anyway. When the world tries to clothe me with the weighty garments of pride, greed, selfishness, and glory, I want to be quick to strip myself of them and stand before God allowing him to clothe me with His worth and value. Today look at yourself in the mirror and ask God to let you see yourself the way He sees you, not the way you see you. Allow Him to show you your worth and your value in being His. The very fact that He sent Jesus to die for you means you are priceless to Him.

for reflection:

- What are the things in your life that you allow to be your identity?
- Are you allowing the things of your past to keep you bound with its labels?
- What "garments" are you wearing that this life has placed on you that are causing you stress, frustration and restlessness?

*On a funny side note, after the surgery was over they wheeled me back into the recovery room and the first thing I said was, "They're bringing sexy back!" Let me tell you, I don't think there was ANYTHING sexy about that moment. That gown, that blue hospital hat, those non-slip socks, that IV, and my droopy sleepy eyes… zero of those things are sexy. But at least I kept my sense of humor. I know my lane, people!

This is a picture of winning as a mom. I let them play with 2x4's and of course they became weapons.

Brayden: "MOM can I go play at Luke and Joey's house?"
Me: "Yes"
Brayden: "Can I bring my axe?"

weapons of warfare

My oldest son changed sports this year from hockey to Jiu Jitsu. My family bleeds hockey since we come from the land of this sport, Minnesota. As soon as it is cold enough to freeze an ice rink, lake, or pond, people are playing hockey on it. This decision may or may not have been difficult for me to let go of. When else was I going to get to yell at other people's kids without getting in trouble for it? I digress. I think teaching a little boy how to fight with supervision and with self-control is important because you never know when they will be in a situation where they will have to defend themselves or someone else. One day at school there was a fight between two boys, and my son came home disappointed because he had been looking for the right position to be able to jump in, take this kid to the ground and stop the fight but didn't know all of the skills yet to do so. I don't think my husband has ever been so proud in his life.

I am sure you have all heard the saying, "You don't bring a knife to a gun fight." My children have mastered the skill of bringing the appropriate weapons to their fights. When you fight in outer space you obviously need to bring an invisible death ray that ONLY works in outer space. When you fight a ninja you need to know karate AND bring a sword because, well, they are ninjas and you have to be prepared for anything. When you fight a Jedi you need to bring a light-saber AND a gun built out of Legos. Appropriate weapons for the fights. As we get older our weapons change and our enemies change, and for some reason we bring our weapons of passive aggression, spite, anger, rage, un-forgiveness, and sarcasm to fights where these weapons actually work AGAINST us instead of FOR us. Not only do we bring the wrong weapons, we are fighting against the wrong "enemy."

It says in Ephesians 6:12 (NLT), *"For we are not fighting against flesh-and-blood enemies, but against evil rulers and*

day three

9

authorities of the unseen world, against mighty powers in this dark world, and against evil spirits in the heavenly places." As if life wasn't hard enough, now we have to deal with an enemy we CAN'T SEE??? Yes, we do, but this isn't the end of the verse. Verses 13-17 tell us what weapons we have to bring to this fight. *"13 Therefore, put on every piece of God's armor so you will be able to resist the enemy in the time of evil. Then after the battle you will still be standing firm. 14 Stand your ground, putting on the belt of truth and the body armor of God's righteousness. 15 For shoes, put on the peace that comes from the Good News so that you will be fully prepared. 16 In addition to all of these, hold up the shield of faith to stop the fiery arrows of the devil. 17 Put on salvation as your helmet, and take the sword of the Spirit, which is the word of God."*

If you will notice, there is only ONE weapon we are given to fight with, and that is the Word of God. This is the only weapon that we need because the Word of God is alive and active and sharper than any two-edged sword. We are given armor to protect us while we are in the fight. The armor keeps our hearts right so we don't get bitter or angry; it protects our thoughts from spiraling out of control; it keeps us going down the right path; it keeps our faith where it needs to be, right in front of us. When it is time to strike we hit with a blow that no enemy can stand against: the very words of God, the creator of the heavens and earth.

This invisible enemy that we are fighting comes to us in the faces of our children, our spouse, people in public, the crazy lady in the carline, our relatives, bosses, or co-workers. So, when you are faced with an ongoing struggle with any of these people, start speaking God's words over the situation. Stop engaging in a war with your words, the silent treatment, or gossip. Choose the weapon that will win the fight.

Pray for God to get involved in the situation. Read your Bible to find out what God says about it. Some battles take longer than others. That's why we were given the "shield of faith" (v. 16), so we can keep standing and keep fighting. This gives us the faith to keep believing that God is already victorious in the most impossible fights. You may not see yourself as a warrior or as strong, but you are. You were created in the likeness and image of God and He is a warrior (Zephaniah 3:17). He created YOU to be a warrior.

for reflection:

- Reflect on the battles that you are fighting right now. Are you fighting them through your own power?
- How can you begin to pray about the situation to get God involved?

"Gabby, why are you crying?"
"BECAUSE I NEED TO HYDRATE!"

power of our words

One summer Jordan and I went to Bellagio, Italy for 7 days and it was glorious! It was the most beautiful place that I have ever been in my life. Jordan was so excited to learn the language because he's SUPER Italian. But me? No, I refused to learn it. What is the point of both of us knowing it? I know German. I don't need to know Italian (judge me all you want for that ignorant statement). One afternoon Jordan thought he was funny and made me go and order myself a bottle of water while we were at the pool. So like a grown up I said, "Challenge accepted" and walked over to the bar. In my mind I was convinced that everybody spoke English so surely this young man knew what I was asking him for. I said, "Can I please have a bottle of water?" He looked at me like a puppy tilting his head as if to say, "I don't understand you." So, almost like a reflex I began pointing at the pool and yelling "WATER! CAN I HAVE A WATER?!!!" He turned around and looked at the pool like, "Is someone drowning?" Then this girl walked over and told him what I was saying, in Italian. He rolled his eyes disgusted at my American ignorance and handed me a bottle of water. All the while Jordan was laughing like a schoolgirl in his chair. I got my water, so I feel like I won.

I would like to believe that I am pretty slick with my words. This has some major downfalls like having to be very aware of the words I use when Jordan and I get into a "heated discussion" because my mouth will get out of control. I read a study that said women say around 20,000 words a day, and I started to wonder what kinds of words was I using? Were a majority of them positive or were a majority of them negative? I learned the development and wiring of the human brain are guided by our experiences during childhood and adolescence.[1] When we as moms use negative and hurtful

day four

words towards our kids it can affect their emotional, cognitive, and social development, and they will actually repeat that behavior towards those around them, which becomes a vicious cycle. We carry a lot of power with just our words. But they aren't "just words." They are seeds that we are planting, not just in our children, but also those around us. How many of us still carry around as truth the hurtful words that were said to us when we were young?

Proverbs 18:21says,"*Death and life are in the power of the tongue, and those who love it will eat its fruits.*" We have the ability to speak life into those around us or we have the ability to speak death over those around us. Something as small as a tongue has the ability to push people to greatness or to cut sharper than a knife. We have each been created in the image and likeness of God, and he spoke everything into existence (except Adam, he made him with his hands, Gen 2:7). It makes sense why our words carry so much power.

We need to be diligent to use the power of our words to build up and not to tear down. In Ephesians 4:29 it says, *"Let no corrupting talk come out of your mouths, but only such as is good for building up, as fits the occasion, that it may give grace to those who hear."* We also need to apply this principle to how we talk about ourselves. We have the ability to kill a dream, kill our own confidence, kill our relationships, kill our joy, kill our peace with our very own words. We need to begin to speak words of life, the Word of God, over ourselves when we are feeling defeated, insecure, afraid, depressed, or angry because God's words bring life not death.

for reflection:

- Are the majority of the words you speak positive or negative? Life-giving or depleting?
- How are you speaking to those around you? Are you building them up or tearing them down?
- How do you speak about yourself?
- What negative words that were spoken to you in your past are you still holding onto?

1.http://www.psychologytoday.com/blog/the-new-brain/201010/sticks-and-stones-hurtful-words-damage-the-brain

"Sammy, why are you barking?
OH! There is a BIRD in the HOUSE????"

these voices in my head
are loud

"Am I crazy? Be honest with me, I feel like I'm crazy..." I can't tell you how many times I asked this question to those closest to me after I had my youngest, Gabby. The youngest two boys really did a number on my sanity, and now I had another baby to care for. I also had to take care of the house, and I was in college, and then there was ministry. I kind of hit a wall and suddenly I was flooded with all of these voices in my head saying, "You're not good enough," "You're fat. Jordan doesn't find you attractive," "NOBODY is going to want to hear from your crazy mouth on a platform," "You're stuck doing this all your life," "Nobody cares what you are doing right now, and it doesn't matter," "You are insignificant," and the comments go on and on and on. The saddest part of this is that I began to believe them. I started to repeat them out of my mouth and they became truth to me.

This was a dark season for me. I felt so bad about myself that I took my frustrations and insecurities out on Jordan and my kids. I felt so stupid verbalizing what was going on in my head because I knew I would sound like a crazy person, but I also recognized that this was an issue that I needed to deal with. When I was first saved I remember reading Battlefield of the Mind by Joyce Meyer, a book which completely changed the way I thought and what thoughts I would allow to take root in my head. I needed to reapply these principals to my life again because my thoughts were wreaking havoc on me and those around me.

In 2 Corinthians 2:5 it says, *"We demolish arguments and every pretension that sets itself up against the knowledge*

day five

of God, and we take captive every thought to make it obedient to Christ." The thoughts that I was thinking did not line up with what God says about me. I was created for a purpose and God has laid it all out for me. None of us are insignificant to Him. *"For we are God's handiwork, created in Christ Jesus to do good works, which God prepared in advance for us to do"* (Ephesians 2:10). Good old Jeremiah 29:11 says, *"'For I know the plans I have for you,' declares the LORD, 'plans to prosper you and not to harm you, plans to give you hope and a future.'"* Hope. He gives us hope so when we are feeling desperate and worthless we can know that these thoughts are not from God. Please look up all of the scriptures below to see what other good things God has to say about you.

We have to get really good at distinguishing between what voices are coming from God and which ones are coming from the enemy. If we allow the enemy to possess space in our head he knows he can make us frustrated, feel defeated, give us anxiety and fear, and all of these things keep us from being the women God has created us to be. We need to stop believing the lies that are fed to us. When a thought pops into your head, quickly ask yourself if that thought is good. If not, then it's not from God. When they are hateful or sorrowful thoughts, immediately counter them with the Word of God. The darkness from the enemy can't stand in the presence of the light of God's truth.

for reflection:

- What lies are you believing about yourself?
- Have you allowed these lies to make a home in your head?
- How have these lies affected your relationships? Your confidence? Your self-worth?
- **Extra Credit:** I encourage you to read *Battlefield of the Mind* by Joyce Meyer.

what God says about you:

- Psalm 139
- Jeremiah 29:11
- Matthew 10:31
- Galatians 2:20
- 1 John 1:9
- Romans 5:6-8
- 2 Corinthians 5:17

"Everyone gets a Glory Ball!"

the honest prayer

Every Wednesday we pray as a staff at church. One Wednesday one of our sweet leaders requested prayer for her grandson because he had a bunch of girls that wanted to date him, and like any grandmother she wanted to protect him from pushy girls. One of my closest friends started to pray for him, and I love listening to her pray because she prays exactly what she is thinking. She said, "I just bind the spirit of skank in the name of Jesus!" I honestly don't remember what else was said after that because I was trying my hardest to suppress my laughter. Here are two reasons I believe God loved that prayer: one, because she was praying from her heart, and two, she was praying with honesty.

God isn't looking for the "holiest" prayer; He is looking for an honest prayer. I think prayer can be really intimating for people because they aren't sure how to pray. Is there a method to it? Will I do it wrong? What if I sound stupid? These were all questions that I used to ask myself. I had a "light bulb moment" when I realized prayer was essentially just talking to God. God wants us to talk to Him all the time, about everything. In 1 Thessalonians 5:17 it says to pray without ceasing. As moms we need to be praying...a lot. God is interesting; he doesn't operate on our timetable, so I realized that I can pray for things in the future and know he hears those prayers too. I pray for my sons' future wives and for my daughter's future husband. I pray for God to show me how to raise my kids so they do what HE created them to do, not what I want them to do. I pray that they will not have a prodigal son or daughter season, and that they will never wander off the path He has designed them to walk down. I pray for the learning differences that they have. I pray for their teachers. I pray for everything because I know God hears my prayers.

I also pray for me. I know that I need God to cover me with grace everyday to make the right choices, to react rationally, and to open my eyes to the things that He wants

day six

me to do in order to be His hands and feet in my everyday life. I make it a point to wake up before the kids to cover my day and theirs with prayer. This is THE most important thing I do every day because it sets the tone of how the rest of my day goes. When I start slipping in my prayer time I feel it. I get irritated easily, frustrated faster, have a hard time making decisions, and I feel empty. This is an area that we all need to maintain daily.

Often times we will forget that prayer and the nearness that we have with Jesus is a gift we have been given. Before Jesus came to Earth, God's people didn't have access to Him like we do today. There was a separation between Him and us because of sin that we couldn't get across. The only remedy that could fix the separation was a perfect sacrifice, and that sacrifice was Jesus. After Jesus had been crucified and the veil was torn (Matthew 27:51) we regained that access to God. He hears YOU when you pray. We need to change our perspectives from we have to pray to we get to pray. Not only do we get to put our needs at his feet we also get to hear from Him. We get access to heavenly answers, ideas, strategies, comfort, peace, joy, and hope when we quiet ourselves in prayer to also listen to Him. He has so much He wants to teach us and tell us, but we need to be willing to listen. This can actually be an art form. We can be so accustomed to moving all day long, that it takes effort to stop, be still, and listen to Him. We need to make time to spend with Jesus, quietly.

I actually have an accountability partner in this area. I found that if I didn't make time to pray before all the kids woke up I wouldn't have time during my day to be quiet and alone with the Lord. We get up at 6:30 am and text each other to make sure we get up. I find my day goes more smoothly, I don't get frustrated as easily, and I can focus better and feel at peace when I make this a priority.

Maybe this is a new concept to you and that is okay! You have to start somewhere, so just open your mouth and talk to Him. You can actually ask Him to teach you how to pray. He wants you to. And He's not looking for something holy, He's looking for something honest.

for reflection:

- How often do you pray?
- Where in your list of priorities does it fall?
- How do you feel after you pray? How do you feel when you forget to pray or go a long time without prayer?
- **Extra credit:** Find a friend who can hold you accountable to pray consistently, and who can pray with you and for you when you are going through trials and difficult times.

" MMOOOOOMMM can you come here and help me make a time machine..."

grace and mercy

How many times have we wanted to just turn back time and undo a mistake or fast forward through a season? I love to watch home improvement shows. They are so convincing! I believed the lie that I too could easily renovate my kitchen. Alone. In one day. Before Jordan got home from work. Let's just say I have made better decisions. I wanted to tear down the backsplash because that is "the easiest part" of demo. I assumed I would need to simply hit it with a hammer and BOOM, like the walls of Jericho it would just fall down. That was not the case. I decided a hammer and a screwdriver would do the trick but all that did was remove the tile AND the sheetrock behind it. At one point I realized I was in too deep to quit so I just starting tearing the wall out. Stepping back and gazing at my ridiculous decision, I looked at the clock and realized my husband was going to be home in 2 hours and would flip out if he saw what I had done. So like any rational person, I packed all of the kids in the car, drove to Home Depot and bought sheetrock to cover the massive hole in my wall. Jordan returned home to what was once a kitchen and was now a demolition zone. This is his life. Please pray for him because he has to put up with me!

I can't tell you how many times I have laid my head down on my pillow at night feeling like a failure and prayed for a redo! That's one of the challenges of being a parent. How do we live in the moment and find joy even when it's hard? How do we let go of criticizing ourselves on all of the "I should haves" that run through our minds? Lamentations 3:22-23 (NLT) says, *"The faithful love of the LORD never ends! His mercies never cease. Great is his faithfulness; his mercies begin afresh each morning."*

day seven

One of the greatest hurdles for me was overcoming the belief that at any moment God was going to come down on a cloud and smite me. That He was up in heaven shaking His head at me regretting His decision to entrust me with these kids. Maybe this is a hurdle for you. The fact is: He loves you. He has equipped you to raise these kids. He extends His mercy and grace towards you every minute of every day. He has everything you need. He is your peace, He is your strength, He is your joy and much of the time He is your sanity.

We are never going to be perfect, and God definitely knows that, and I know that I need His grace every second of every day. I think we need to stop trying to be perfect because it is too much pressure. We also need to give ourselves some grace. I have a friend who was at the mall with her son when he was just a baby. He was getting hungry, so she gave him a french fry box to chew on until they could get him something to eat. An older woman walked by her and said, "You can do better, mom." This comment really hurt her! This was not okay to say to a mom who is trying to do the best thing in that moment. I have been there; we have all been there. What she needed in that moment was grace. Let's all get really good at extending grace towards each other and to ourselves because God always extends it to us.

When we are feeling defeated, when we are feeling like we are messing everything up, this is the perfect moment for us to go to God and ask Him to flood us with His grace and mercy. The good news is that His grace and mercy never run out, even when ours does.

for reflection:

- In what areas of your life do you need grace?
- What are you really hard on yourself about?
- How do you handle feeling defeated?

new terrain

I went through boot camp from October through December in Great Lakes, Illinois. If you are familiar with the north, this is the time when it starts snowing and it doesn't stop until March. In boot camp we marched everywhere we went no matter the conditions outside. They would just have us wear a rain jacket if it was raining and a heavy jacket if it was snowing. I was very accustomed to the snow and the ice. In fact it is a fine art to know how to walk on the ice, an art not many people in my boot camp division knew anything about. For the first week after the roads iced over we would be marching in ranks to a cadence, so everyone would be marching at the same pace, and then I would see people slip and fall out of ranks. Even though people fell down, the division wouldn't stop marching. We would keep going and they had to catch back up with the group. It was actually one of the most amusing things I have seen. Have you ever seen grown people fall down? Some of them could have won an Oscar for their performances.

They fell because they were not familiar with this new terrain. They had never walked on this kind of ground before, but they learned quickly by watching those around them and by personal experience how to navigate the ice. Motherhood is most certainly new terrain. We can read all of the books, ask all of the questions, but until we are in it ourselves we have no idea what we are doing. How we navigate this new terrain is extremely important. We may fall and we will make mistakes, but the most important thing to do is to get back up because life does not stop moving forward.

After 40 years in the desert, Moses died and the responsibility to take the Israelites into the Promised land

day eight

was given to Joshua. This was a whole new experience for Joshua. He had never led the people in this capacity before and now he was the one to take them into what God had promised them. This was new terrain for all of them, but in Joshua 1:5 God says, *"No one will be able to stand against you all the days of your life. As I was with Moses, so I will be with you; I will never leave you nor forsake you."* God wasn't leading them into new terrain just to leave them to fend for themselves. The Ark of the Covenant, which represents the presence of God, went before them and when He went before them they were victorious.

When you go from season to season and from new terrain to new terrain God will lead you and guide you. He will never leave you nor forsake you. He doesn't lead us into new seasons for us to fend for ourselves. He goes before us. I have had to navigate going from 1 to 2 to 3 to 4 kids, and every time people would ask me, "What are you going to do with all these kids?"My answer every time was "I don't know, sell one?" but God helped me every step of the way. In Joshua 3:4, Joshua is talking to the Israelites and says, *" Then you will know which way to go, since you have never been this way before..."* I have not had to step into the terrain of having a teenager yet, but I know God will be in that season too so that I don't slap the sass out of my kids' mouths. This life is a series of walking from season to season. Whatever season you are in right now ask God to lead you through the tough terrain. He is faithful to provide.

Maybe you are a mom without support and this is very frustrating and lonely terrain for you. God is with you. Maybe you have been blessed to be a new mom in a blended family and you are trying to navigate how to be a mother to children that are not biologically yours. God will give you wisdom. Maybe you recently had a baby and you have NO idea what you are doing because all of those books lied to you. God will give you peace. Maybe all of your kids have moved out of the house and you are questioning what to do now. God will give you direction. In every season God is with you, will lead you, and will give you direction. Don't lose heart. Your best days are ahead of you!

for reflection:

- What tough terrain have you tried to navigate before that caused you to fall?
- Have you asked God to go before you in each season that you have walked through?

Dominic: "Mom drinks coffee and eats soup and chicken."

Asher: "She eats pickles too."

If I were an unrelated eavesdropper I would think their mother is 80...

uniqueness

When I finally decided to live my life for Christ I had a sort of life crisis. I was used to being loud and extremely sarcastic, I drank a lot, I looked for the approval of men, I was extremely angry, I smoked, and I cussed like a sailor (because, I literally was a sailor). I knew if I wanted to live according to His word then I would need to change, but all of the women I knew who were Christians knitted, baked and were soft spoken. I was able to do ZERO of these things. I tried to bake. I was awful. I knew that I didn't want to knit so I didn't even try. And I tried to be soft spoken, but the people in my life thought that there was something wrong with me and told me that I should go see a doctor.

So, I felt like I was failing at being a Christian because I didn't fit the 'mold.' I read a bunch of books about being a woman of God but none of it described me. All of this was so foreign to me and I began to think, "If I can't fit in as a Christian, maybe I don't belong here." So God and I had a conversation. It went something like this:

"God I have so many issues. I don't fit into a mold. Who am I supposed to be? Do I have to wear a floor length skirt? Can I wear makeup? Do I have to bake? I don't really like people; do I need to be around them? Can I please have friends under 40 that are also Christians? Do I have to be soft spoken? Am I allowed to watch regular TV or do I have to just watch the Christian channel? Why am I here?"

Then, after my meltdown and the ugly cry, God responded....His response was laughter. Have you ever heard God laugh? It's comforting, yet terrifying. And because I learn best by watching, not necessarily listening, He showed

day nine

me that we are not meant to fit a mold. He brought into my life many different types of women of all ages who don't fit into any mold. Some of them are loud and boisterous. Some of them are calm and collected. Some of them are super fashionable and some of them don't care about fashion at all. Some of them have gone to college and some of them have never finished high school. But we all have one thing in common: we all love the Lord and we all serve Him. He has created all of us to do different things with unique gifts and talents, and that is what makes all of us beautiful.

Psalm 139:13-18 says, *"13 For you created my inmost being; you knit me together in my mother's womb. 14 I praise you because I am fearfully and wonderfully made; your works are wonderful, I know that full well. 15 My frame was not hidden from you when I was made in the secret place, when I was woven together in the depths of the earth. 16 Your eyes saw my unformed body; all the days ordained for me were written in your book before one of them came to be. 17 How precious to me are your thoughts, God! How vast is the sum of them! 18 Were I to count them, they would outnumber the grains of sand—when I awake, I am still with you."*

I want you to read these verses over and over until it sinks deep into your heart. These verses tell a beautiful story of each of us, and how God has created you. God is the mastermind behind who you are and what you are created to do. Throughout the Bible there are stories of women who did different things for God. Esther was a queen who saved the Israelites (Esther 1-9); Deborah was a warrior who fought armies (Judges 4-5); Mary was the mother of Jesus (Luke 1:26-38), and there are many more women throughout the Bible. Like these women who had unique gifts, God has created you with a purpose and He has a beautiful plan for your life too.

Often the world around us will try to tell us who we need to be and what we need to look like, and if we don't fit into that mold we are told we don't belong. We all desperately want to belong, so in order to belong we might do drastic things, and slowly we lose our hope that there is anything else for us. We feel broken and empty. But none of these things will ever fill that emptiness. Until we realize that we belong to God and He always accepts us we will never feel complete. For those of you who believe you were a mistake and God has nothing for you, you have believed a lie. God doesn't make mistakes. Period.

Because of Jesus we all belong to God's family, and that makes all of us family. And families are made up of many unique people. I know mine is, and God does this on purpose. When we all come together with our different gifts and talents we paint a beautiful picture of who God is. He is smart, funny, creative, kind, loving, honest, beautiful, forgiving, selfless, strong... He is unique. Just like you!

So, yes, some women bake and that's a gift that they have been given. Yes, some women knit and some women are soft spoken. That is how they have been made. Me, I like my eyes and I am funny. I am merciful and a good storyteller. And I actually like to bake now, but I'm still not soft spoken and probably never will be. But I have gifts that make me unique and I am ok with that because that's how God has created me. Don't compare yourself to someone else. When we do that we are saying, "Who I am and how I was created isn't good enough." God made you beautiful and you will ALWAYS be good enough for Him. Don't be afraid to say nice things about yourself. Don't be afraid to say that you are good at something; these are all gifts that have been given to you.

for reflection:

- What are you good at?
- What are some gifts that you have been given? Spend some time thinking about that and write it down.

Gabby wanted wings, so we bought her wings.
This is Gabby crying because she couldn't really fly after she put them on.

While watching an episode of The Voice a contestant finished singing their song and Brayden said, "I wonder what it would be like to get booed, like if they just told them to get off the stage..."

dreams

I wish I were a singer. I wish I could do runs like singers can do. When I try it sounds like I'm helplessly looking for a note. It's not pretty. I love to stand in the front row of church and sing as loud as I can pretending to sing as well as our worship team, but I promise you they turn the music up to drown me out. This desire has gotten so intense that I have dreamed about trying out for the worship team. In my dream I was in the same room as our worship leader and I thought if they overheard me singing they would definitely want me on the team, so I sang as passionately as I could. When I was finished the worship leader looked at me and said, "WOW! That was....loud..." I couldn't even make the team in my dream! That's pretty bad.

Do you have dreams in your heart that you don't see how they are going to happen in the season you are in right now? This season doesn't last forever. If your kids are small and require a lot of your attention right now you don't need to allow those dreams to die. In this season bathe those dreams in prayer, because when/if it's time for them to happen, God will make them happen and your heart will be ready. Or if your kids are older and you feel like you missed your window, I want to remind you that Abraham had a child at 100 years old. There is no expiration date on God's ability to make your dreams come to pass.

Each and every one of you has a significant call in your life. You were each created with a purpose and for a purpose. Being a mother is not a roadblock, it's actually a launching pad. As mothers our capacity grows; we learn patience, we learn perseverance (because a 3 year old that covers himself in body butter will NOT cause me to lose my

day ten

salvation), we learn to love in ways we never knew was possible, we learn to communicate in ways we never knew we could communicate, we learn humility (because there is nothing sexy about having poop on your shirt) and a host of other skills I don't think we would have learned as quickly as motherhood teaches us.

I remember having the dream to go to college. No one in my family had graduated from college and I wanted to reach that goal. After having three kids and being pregnant with a fourth, I didn't think it would ever happen - until God reminded me of the dream and I said, "It's now or never." So I started taking classes online when I was 8 months pregnant and I graduated in May of 2014. I am glad I completed college so my kids could see what it looks like to work hard in school and to work hard to reach a goal. It is important for you to continue to dream in all stages of your life. Your kids aren't always going to be under your roof. What are you going to do when they move out? Start dreaming and praying now.

I encourage you to write all of the dreams you have down in a journal. Some of these dreams may not happen for years, but don't stop dreaming and hearing from the Lord about how to get yourself ready for what He has for you. You can start reading books about the dreams He has placed in you. Don't give them up! God has a plan and a purpose for your life and it may not stop at being a mother. It says in Ephesians 2:10, *"For we are God's handiwork, created in Christ Jesus to do good works, which God prepared in advance for us to do."* Maybe you feel called to politics or to education or to ministry. God wants to use YOU to make His name famous wherever you go and in whatever you do. However, I don't want you to neglect the season that you are in right now. What you are doing right now by raising your kids is extremely important. You have little (and maybe some of you have big) people watching you. Let them watch you dream and set goals. Let them see you pray for your future. These are seeds that you are planting in them so they know what to do with their dreams someday.

for reflection:

- What dreams do you have in your heart?
- What is preventing you from accomplishing your dreams?
- Have you allowed the part in you that dreams to die? Pray for God to re-awaken it.

Gabby: "Mommy, you got a big butt,
I got a little butt..."
Me: "Don't say things like that, but you are correct..."

health

"Random question, any interest in helping out on a TV shoot tomorrow? It's for my friend's new show." "I would LOVE to! That would be so much fun." Famous last words, it was NOT so much fun. I arrived at a cycling studio, dressed in my work out clothes to appear like I am working out, because that's what we are doing, pretending... right? WRONG! I knew this was not pretend as soon as they locked my cycling shoes into the peddles and the lady put her head set on, explained how the bikes worked, then began to yell at us.

When I do something I go all in. I play for keeps and for some reason this scenario was no different. What made it worse was a huge TV screen that had the stats of each cyclist and how they were performing, and my bike number was NOT going to be at the bottom of that list! Did I mention that there was a camera on us the whole time filming this? About 15 minutes into this workout I knew I was in way over my head. I became light headed and felt like throwing up. Because I was locked into my bike I was certain the poor girl in front of me was going to get thrown up on, but since she was the one who locked me into my bike I guess it would be pay back. There was a little break in the filming and in the most casual manner possible (despite my panic) I asked, "How do I get out of these peddles?" They must have heard the desperation in my voice because one girl almost fell off her bike trying to get me off mine. I stumbled into the lobby and asked a blurry guy where the bathroom was and he pointed to a wall of doors. I chose one, closed the door, and was confused when there was not a toilet in the room.... oh, because it was a shower. So I stumbled back out into the lobby, found an actual bathroom, and immediately lay on the floor. I know that is so unsanitary and gross, but I wanted to voluntarily lie down instead of passing out. I knew at this moment I was very out of shape and had not made my health a priority.

day eleven

I started to spiral, asking myself, "Why did I eat all of those chili cheese burritos when I was pregnant with Gabby?""Why do I not drink enough water?""I should not have eaten that Chicken Caesar wrap for lunch because it tastes super gross coming back up.""Why did I say yes to this?""I'm sure it's all of the GMOs. I don't even know what that stands for but I think they are bad."

Mothers are notorious for putting everything before themselves. It's what we do instinctively. This experience taught me a priceless lesson: I can't take care of other people when I'm not taking care of myself, and this includes my physical health. I need to make time to be healthy, not to fit into a smaller jean size(although that would be a great side effect), but so I can be around for a long time. I started to notice how tired I always was, how late I went to bed, how I snacked right before I went to sleep, and how I had zero desire to work out and would put it off every day. I also noticed how I couldn't focus or think as sharply as I would like. I needed to make a change in my health not just because my kids deserve better, but because I deserve better.

Maybe you are in the same boat. Maybe you have let your health be put on the back burner because you have been busy doing what moms do… everything. I encourage you; it's not too late to start now. I'm not talking about going to the extreme, but to make a conscious decision to put your health first. It takes time to retrain your thinking and to make it a habit, but did you know it only takes 21 days to form a habit?

1 Corinthians 3:16 says, *"Do you not know that you are God's temple and that God's Spirit dwells in you?"* I'm not saying we need to put pressure on ourselves to look like a Victoria's Secret model, but if we are trying to be the hands and feet of Christ, we need to make sure the vehicle is taken care of so we can be as effective as possible. Hear me; this is not to place shame on you. None of us were created to look the same and that is intentional. What we can control is our health. What God has created you to do is significant, and we need to take care of ourselves so we can carry it out.

for reflection:

- Have you put taking care of your health on hold?
- What is one thing you can do today to make a healthy choice?
- Who in your life can you ask to hold you accountable?
- **Extra credit:** Find a partner to join you on this journey so you can inspire each other

*Asher: "MOM, Calvin farted on my food
at lunch today!"
Dominic: "Did he mean to?"*

*My first question is: how does one NOT mean
to fart on a person's food?*

blinking isn't the same thing
as sleep

When we were getting ready to launch our church I was given the privilege of leading the kids' ministry. To make sure we were going into this new season with as much insight and wisdom as possible, Jordan and I were sent to Austin, TX to see how they were doing their mobile kids' church. We were so excited because this was a little overnight getaway and an opportunity to learn something new. On our way to Austin I started feeling like I was getting sick and about an hour in we had to pull over because I had started feeling so ill and I needed medication immediately. I assumed it was just allergies, but this was not the case. I went to bed that night heavily medicated and we debated whether to go to the church the next morning or not. But I am not a quitter, so I took some pills and pushed through. The team we met was amazing. They were so willing to teach us anything we wanted to know and share their wisdom with us. One of the tips they gave me was to make sure we mark the laptops with the kids' ministry name so they weren't lost or misplaced. Being probably too medicated at this point I decided to respond with, "I'll just pee on them." It was one of those moments where I heard the words leave my mouth but it was too late, it was out there. The air went awkwardly silent and one of the guys walked away. Maybe we shouldn't have gone that morning after all.

We get so used to running at 100% all the time that we can forget to rest. We can take care of other people before we take care of ourselves, but eventually it will catch up to us. It will come in the form of sickness, anxiety, depression, or any number of ailments. We need to make sure we are

day twelve

making time to rest. Some days I have to be okay with the fact that all of the dishes didn't get done. I have to be ok with toys being on the floor. I have to be ok with the laundry not getting done and I have to be okay with unplugging from my phone and computer. If any of these things do not get done the world isn't going to stop spinning. My kids aren't going to feel unloved, and my husband isn't going to ask me why the house isn't clean (because he is a smart man). If my mental and physical health aren't in order, my life isn't in order.

I would like to take a minute and speak to the single moms. I was raised by a single mom. I respect and admire her so much and attribute who I am today to her. I remember watching how hard it was on her to do it alone, and I wish she had spent more time resting. I encourage you to pull some women around you who can relieve you from your non-stop job once a week for a couple of hours so you can rest. I know it can be hard to ask for help, but you need rest. And moms who have help: I encourage you to reach out to the single moms and help them feel supported and remembered. In Hebrews 4:9-11 it says, *"There remains, then, a Sabbath-rest for the people of God; [10] for anyone who enters God's rest also rests from their works, just as God did from his. [11] Let us, therefore, make every effort to enter that rest, so that no one will perish by following their example of disobedience."*

None of us know what we are doing, and women are watching you to see how you do any number of tasks throughout your day to see if they can use your strategies or ideas. Women need to see that rest is important to you and that you make an intentional effort to unplug. Unfortunately, we can make motherhood look awful because we are always tired and have very little energy to do anything productive. It's because we are running on empty. Pull out your calendar today and block off one day every week where you will rest. Let the people in your life know this is the day you are going to unplug so they know not to call you, email you, or want to meet with you for dinner. Make time for rest, otherwise all of the "free time" you have on your calendar will fill up and you will be left feeling depleted and tired. Make time for you!

for reflection:

- What are some things in your life you can lay down to make time for yourself to rest?
- How often do you unplug from your phone, social media, and errands to recharge?

"Daddy, drive fast like mommy..."

laughter

Minnesota is a fascinating place to my kids. It snows there. Like, a lot. We will go every other year for Christmas and each time they can't wait to go to the sliding hill. My oldest son learned very quickly NOT to trust his uncle when he says things like, "Trust me, this is super fun." When he was 4 years old he walked his tiny self up the hill, excited just to get to the top. His uncle put him on an inner tube (if you are familiar with sledding you know the inner tube is for professional sledders ONLY), and pushed him as hard as he could down the hill. This would have been perfectly acceptable if there hadn't been a ramp at the bottom of the hill, launching his tiny body into the air like a flailing missile. A normal parent would have gone running down the hill to make sure their child was ok. I on the other hand did not do that. For some reason this made me laugh harder than I have laughed in a long time. This whole scene looked like something you would see in a cartoon. Yes, there were tears (mine were from laughing and my sons were from fear), but everyone was ok because in Minnesota you wear so many layers when you go outside they act as a form of bulletproof outerwear.

Being a mom can be challenging and we can get so caught up in the day-to-day routine that after a while we forget when the last time we laughed was. I LOVE to laugh; it's probably one of my favorite things to do. I was raised in a family where that is what we did a majority of the time; tell stories and jokes and laugh. However, there was a time after I had my third son that I stopped laughing. I became depressed and the heaviness of life began to wear on me. I became more familiar with what yelling sounded like than what my laugh sounded like. This was not a very pleasant time in my marriage either because I had lost who I was and found very little joy in anything. I had a moment when I saw what I was doing to the relationships around me and I made a conscious decision to change it. I hadn't taken it to God before because I didn't realize that I had drifted. I finally took it to the Lord and continually asked for Him to help me, to take me from this dark place and set my feet on solid ground again. It didn't happen overnight; I had to fight for surrender daily and I still have to be aware of my mental state. But I have been set free from that bondage. If you are in this place in your life I want you to know you can find joy again. You can laugh again. You don't have to stay stuck in this place.

Proverbs 17:22 says, *"A cheerful heart is good medicine, but a crushed spirit dries up the bones."* Apparently there is some science behind the truth of this scripture, go figure! I looked up the effects that laughter has on us and I found a list of 10 reasons why laughing is good for you:

1. It decreases stress
2. It helps coping skills
3. It improves blood pressure and flow
4. It provides a burst of exercise
5. It impacts blood sugar levels
6. It helps manage pain
7. It boosts your social skills
8. It reduces aggression
9. It energizes organs
10. It boosts the immune system

I believe that Jesus laughed. I will speak specifically about Matthew 19:14 where Jesus says, *"Let the little children come to me, and do not hinder them, for the kingdom of heaven belongs to such as these."* Kids are drawn to joy and to laughter. Just watch them; they naturally gravitate toward happy things. I don't think Jesus was weeping when He spoke these words to His disciples. I know we all imagine Him on the cross, or flipping over tables, or as a baby in a manger, but he had a personality. He had a sense of humor and laughed.

I encourage you to laugh. Some seasons we go through can be hard and it can be very challenging to find something to laugh about, but try. Sit at a park and just watch people. People are crazy (especially kids because they fall down a lot). You will quickly find yourself laughing. Don't take yourself or life too seriously. I think it's important for us to be able to laugh at ourselves. One last scripture that paints a beautiful picture of laughter and its place in our life is Proverbs 31:35, *"She is clothed with strength and dignity; she can laugh at the days to come."* Yesterday, today, and tomorrow have no authority to grip you with anxiety or fear. Our security lies in the authority of Christ, and this gives us confidence so we can feel secure enough to laugh.

for reflection:

- When is the last time that you laughed?
- If you aren't laughing, why not?
- What in your life is preventing you from laughing?

Me: "We don't say that we hate people!"
Brayden: "Well, I don't hate her I just don't like her at all."

friendships matter

Every week I would go over to my friend Amanda's house and have coffee and let our kids play. One week I was sitting at the table and Amanda was in the kitchen when another friend walked in with her kids. When Amanda went over to greet her, the friend's 4-year-old daughter looked at Amanda and said, "Mrs. Amanda? Do you have a vagina?" This was one of those moments when the air is sucked out of the room because you aren't certain what the acceptable response is to this question. My go-to response is uncomfortable nervous laughter, so I went with that one. Laughter filled the air and this little girl soon got distracted by all the other kids and moved on, but that was a close one.

I can't tell you how thankful I am for the friends I have in my life. They have hugged me while I cried, prayed for me when I felt hopeless, let me rant about incredibly unimportant things, spoken life into me, and believed the best in me. We have spent hours laughing at the most ridiculous things and I'm pretty sure there have been a couple of times when I have peed a little from laughing so hard. These women are a strength in my life that I would never want to lose. I have had my good moments and my bad moments around them and they still love me.

The longer I am a mom the more I realize I need friends in my life. Jordan is definitely my best friend (because he sees me naked and still loves me), but there is something special about having girlfriends who have gone through seasons like I have and can relate to the weird thoughts that go on in my head. I saw a quote from Bill Murray that said, "Friendship is so weird. You just pick a human you've met and you're like 'yup, I like this one' and you just do stuff with them." This pretty much sums up how friendships begin. Friendships make us feel normal when the only things we have become accustomed to are kids crying, spitting up on us, and asking us for food.

day fourteen

David had a friendship that resembled a brother's relationship with King Saul's son, Jonathan. After David killed Goliath he was brought before King Saul, still holding Goliath's head, and from that day on Jonathan and David were best friends (1 Samuel 18). If they had BFF necklaces back then those two would totally have had them. I'm not sure what did it for them; the fact that David, a child who stepped up and killed the most feared enemy with a slingshot (every boy's dream come true), or the fact that David carried Goliath's head with him to speak to the king. Either way Jonathan thought, "He is one of my people; we need to hang out." David and Jonathan fought together, they learned together, and they were inseparable. They thought alike and they made each other stronger. It says in Proverbs 27:17, *"as iron sharpens iron so one person sharpens another."*

My friends make me stronger. Their hearts break when mine does. They support me, but they are also quick to keep me accountable if I drift. We need these people in our lives. We don't have to have a ton of friends, but we do need ones that are trustworthy and will love us when our walls are down. Friendships will also go through seasons. Some are closer than others, but they never truly go away. That's the mark of a true friend; being able to go months without speaking, then pick up right where you left off when you are together again. Friendships are a two way street though, and we need to invest in our friends with our time, words of encouragement, wise counsel, and an empathetic ear.

Place your friendships on your priority list. They are there as a support system for you. God intended us to have them in our lives. Jesus even had 3 disciples (friends) that were the closest to him. They saw Him cry, they saw Him on the Mt. of Transfiguration, they saw Him turn water into wine, and they ate with Him. Maybe you don't have very many friends or all of your friends are in such different seasons in life that you can't relate to one another anymore. I encourage you to step out of your comfort zone and invest some of your precious time in cultivating friendships. It's worth it.

for reflection:

- Who are the women in your world that you would call "real friends"?
- How are you making investments in those "real friends"?
- Are there women you spend your time with that tear you down and make you feel bad about yourself? You may want to begin to distance yourself from them.

These are the faces of kids OVERJOYED about being at the World's Greatest Animal Exhibit.

Jordan:"Whose car do you want to take?"
Me: "I don't care"
Jordan:"It sounds like you don't want us to take your car"
Me: "I NEVER want to take my car anywhere.
It smells like feet and Chuck E. Cheese"

life is an adventure

Every summer I pack up the kids and drive to Minnesota for 2 weeks. It's a very long drive but I think I have it down to a science. I got some portable DVD players that rotate through the car. I buy small activities to give to each kid every two hours so they have something new to do, and we stop...a LOT. One particular summer I was driving through Oklahoma and I saw a sign advertising "The World's Greatest Animal Exhibit." I thought, "Why not? I'm sure this is legit." We all piled out of the car and paid WAY too much for a ticket to enter. I'm not certain why they didn't have a tour guide, but the only thing separating us from a bear, a lion, or an alligator was a chain link fence. I kid you not; there was a legitimate Liger at this place. The kids thought it was cool to be able to get that close to the animals, and at the end of the tour they asked if the kids wanted to play with a baby white tiger in its cage! You only live once, right? Thankfully the tiger didn't rip their faces off and it made for an amazing memory for the kids. Then when we got to Iowa I let the boys pee in a cornfield because that's what you do.

That summer I wanted to make sure we went on as many adventures as possible. That is how I also want to approach life, as an adventure, because we are only given one life and I want to make it count. There are so many people just shuffling through life, but at the end of mine I want to say I saw things, made things, did things, and finished things. I used to see having kids as a hindrance to doing all of that until it dawned on me that I would either be putting life on hold until they all left the house OR I could bring them along on the journey. If they see me doing things, when they grow up they will be inspired to do things too. In John 10:10 (NLT) it says, *"The thief's purpose is to steal and kill and destroy. My purpose is to give them a rich and satisfying life."* I never wanted to go in

day fifteen

public with them because I was constantly doing a head count or worrying that we would be inconveniencing people with how many kids we had. Now I don't care if people are inconvenienced because we choose to teach our kids how to behave in public, and if that means they have a melt down and we use that as a teaching lesson, then so be it. I got sick of being a prisoner inside my house, so now I bring my circus into public and let them experience life.

God has blessed us all with this life and he wants us to live the heck out of it. Have you always wanted to climb a mountain? Do it. Have you always wanted to travel? Do it. Have you always wanted to write a book? Do it. Have you always wanted to act? Find an amateur acting class and do it. Have you wanted to learn how to dance? Do it (be careful of the classes that have the stripper poles in the room; those classes might not be what you are looking for... or maybe it is). I'm not a huge fan of the phrase "the glory days" because I think every day can be a glory day. Every year can be a glory year. Life doesn't come to an end when you reach 30. You don't suddenly have to check yourself into a senior living community and eat soft food for the rest of your life. Every season of life won't be easy or fun, but every season can be an adventure. Our perspective just needs to change, because a lot of times our perspective affects our attitude toward things. You can ask yourself: *What did I learn? What did I do? What did I see? Who did I meet? Where did I go? What's next?* This season of staying home with my kids is a little less spontaneous and wild as it once was, but it's a different kind of adventure. And when I look back on it I want to say I had fun and I am a better person because of it. I also want my kids to be able to look back on their lives having experienced adventures.

for reflection:

- How do you perceive your life?
- What have you always wanted to do but haven't yet?
- What can you modify to bring your kids along for the ride?

"Mom I learned that our toilet water is what people in Galveston drink...no really, it's a fact..."

the throne of your heart

When I was in the Navy I was a Search and Rescue Swimmer, and I had to go through 4 weeks of intense training in Jacksonville, Florida. One of the last tests that we had to take was a night swim in the St. Johns River. This river feeds right into the ocean and many different creatures live in it; most of which will eat you. When we did open water swims like this we had a swimming buddy, and since I was the smallest one in the class, I was in the front to set the pace. Because this test was at night, it was much more difficult than the others had been. We were to follow our instructor who only had a chemical light attached to his snorkel for us to see him. This would have been no problem if there weren't any other lights on the water, but we were swimming towards a bridge with many, many lights on it.

I was swimming my heart out, assuming I was following the light on my instructor's snorkel, until I heard him in the boat behind us screaming at me, "WHERE ARE YOU GOING?" I stopped swimming, looked up, and saw that I had swum away from the rest of the group because I was swimming toward a light on the bridge not toward the instructor's light. I immediately played the scene from Jaws in my head and started freaking out as I tried to swim at lightning speed back to the group. If a shark was to happen upon us my hope was that it would choose a bigger person.

What are we following, and what are we allowing to lead us? For the longest time I was following what felt good and what I thought was right until I surrendered my life to God. I put so many different things on pedestals as idols and made those things my guide. I would put my pride on a throne. I would put worldly success on a throne. I would put recognition

day sixteen

on a throne. I would put my friendships on a throne. I would put my husband or my kids on a throne. These were all things that I allowed to dictate what I focused my attention on. These were things that I would invest all my time in and passion into. All these things were idols in my life and I put every single one on the throne of my heart, where only God belonged.

We can get so busy focusing our attention on the wrong things; making idols of things that will always be insignificant compared to God. When we focus all our attention and efforts on things and people, our focus gets off track and our hearts start to drift from where they need to be, Jesus. He is the only one that has the right to the throne of our heart. He is the one who made it possible to live a life surrendered to Him. We need to be extremely sensitive to the things that we have put before God. Anything can be an idol: pride, sex, motherhood, being a wife, titles, money or possessions, anger, alcohol or drugs, fear, friendships, dreams, TV, food...anything. While being a mother or a wife, having friends, money, a good paying job, or many possessions are all gifts from God, we should never take what has been given as a blessing and place it before the One who blesses.

Matthew 22:37 says, *"Jesus replied: 'Love the Lord your God with all your heart and with all your soul and with all your mind.'"* We need to love God more than anything else because nothing else can answer our prayers; nothing else can love us like He can; nothing else can give us hope, life, or peace like He can. Everything pales in comparison to Him and His love for us. Jesus gives us this command to protect us from drifting, to protect us from becoming slaves to the things of this world.

for reflection:

- What are the things you put before God?
- What are the things you follow before you follow God?
- Have you surrendered all of the worldly things you hold tightly to, into God's hands?
- **Extra Credit:** Read *Pursuit of God* by A. W. Tozer

"I can't be Wonder Woman without my skirt!!!"

balance

"Mrs. Mauriello, we are calling to see if you were on your way to pick up your boys from school?" and "Mrs. Mauriello, we were wondering if you were able to pick up Dominic today since it's raining?" These questions were what the voicemails asked after I got home from picking up the kids from school. Like all organized mothers I forgot that this particular day was a half-day and it was raining. Two of my boys go to an elementary school and my oldest goes to an intermediate school. They get out at different times. When I realized it was a half-day I rushed out of the house to pick them up...in my pajamas. Not the cute pajamas that could look like casual wear, the pajamas that are bright red and have mosquitoes all over them. Yes, I own those, and they were a gift from my mother because she is hilarious. I also forgot my phone. I noticed that it was raining outside and I didn't want my oldest son to have to walk home in the rain, so I thought, "Oh easy, I'll jump in the carline and pick him up." *Wrong!* The carline was so backed up that by the time I got to the front, Dominic was gone and I didn't have my phone to call the office to tell them that I was picking him up, AND I was already 10 minutes late picking up the younger boys. Since I was that late I had to go into the office to pick them up. *In my pajamas!* I'm not sure who was more horrified: the office staff, my boys, or me. I got home to a very angry boy who was freezing and soaking wet. I wouldn't say this was a winning day for me.

We have to get really good at multi-tasking and balancing our lives. I think this is actually a gift given to us because we are responsible for not losing, hurting, or breaking our kids. Our capacity has to expand to get things done for not only us, but for those who depend on us. One thing that God shared with me this year was that our ability to compartmentalize our lives was actually not healthy. We will put on different hats for different things, trying to be different people at different times, and this is a really schizophrenic way of living. After a while we forget who we are supposed to be at any given time and it puts pressure on us to perform, being different people all day long.

This was the only way I knew how to live my life until this year. It would make me frustrated and it mentally exhausted me. I couldn't be all of these different people all day long. My focus and alignment were off. My life looked like this diagram:

And if I was busy being a mother most of the day I wouldn't have enough time for God, or to be a wife, or to be a pastor, and I would always feel so defeated and unaccomplished. Then God showed me what it should look like with this diagram:

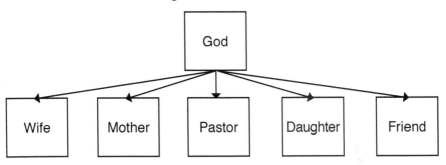

Out of the time that I spend with him every day I can be all of these things, and I don't have to change who I am for each role. Philippians 4:12-13 says, *"I know what it is to be in need, and I know what it is to have plenty. I have learned the secret of being content in any and every situation, whether well fed or hungry, whether living in plenty or in want. 13 I can do all this through him who gives me strength."* My approach as a pastor is different than my approach to being a mother, but my personality and nature don't change. My peace doesn't change, because who I am is found in Him, and what I do flows from who I am in Him. This has brought so much peace into my life. I don't go to sleep feeling like I have failed all day long. My focus will change from day to day, but I don't have to change who I am in the process.

for reflection:

- Have you been living your life compartmentalized?
- How has it made you feel at the end of the day?
- What would your life look like if everything you did flowed from your time with God?

standing watch

Standing watch was something that was mandatory while I was in the Navy. The watch post I hated the most was when the ship was out to sea and I had to stand alone on the back of the ship in the cold and dark. I would have to stand back there for *four hours* and wasn't allowed to leave until someone came to replace me. It was the worst. But it was necessary because my job was to watch for any potential threats and report them to the bridge (from where the ship is driven and steered, and where the captain is). In a sense, I was responsible for keeping the people that were onboard safe from any danger. If I had fallen asleep I would have potentially allowed harm to come to my fellow sailors; so I had to stay awake and stay vigilant, no matter how boring it was.

This picture couldn't be any more accurate for the position of a mother. I have had seasons where I don't feel like I am contributing much to this family or to society. This is how I felt standing on the back of that ship. I would wonder, "What am I even doing?" or "What is the point of this?"I will sometimes get my worth and value confused with receiving a paycheck or with praise from people. I hear the debate that seems to be ongoing about the worth and value of a stay-at-home mom, and it makes me angry that people have been categorized by their contribution to the economy or to the work force.

Moms have been given a post to stand watch over our families. We are up late during nights with sick kids, reading books that are awful, planning meals, going to birthday parties for our kids' classmates...So *many* birthday parties! And we rarely hear "Thank you" for the things we do.

But these things are extremely necessary. We are guardians of our kids' hearts. We have the power to speak life into our children. We are role models. We are who our daughters want to be when they grow up, and we are setting the bar for whom our sons will want to marry one day.

While these seasons seem daunting and we can often feel unappreciated, wondering if anything we are doing matters, I want to remind you that God chose you to be this child's mother. Out of all the women in the world, He chose you. Much like Mary was chosen to be the mother of Jesus (Luke 1:38). God does not take this role lightly, as even Jesus needed a mother. If He chose you, then He equipped you to stand this watch. *"She sets about her work vigorously; her arms are strong for her tasks"* (Proverbs 31:17).

Like all watches, the ones we are standing will come to an end. Our kids grow up so fast, and we only have so long with them to train them up in the way that they should go (Proverbs 22:6). Then they are on their own to live the lives God created them to live. No watch that is stood is pointless; they are about protecting people. We are raising and protecting God's children. These kids need us to stay vigilant and awake. Do not fall asleep on your watch.

for reflection:

- How have you approached the responsibility of being a mother?
- Do you see it as a burden?
- What changes can you make to ensure you stay at your post and stay vigilant until you are relieved?

Me: "When you grow up you'll get married and be such
a good mommy."
Gabby: "Yeah I'll have my family. Then they die"
Me: "WHAT! No, they aren't going to die!"
Gabby: "Yes they do. People die, Mom."
Me: "When we get old, yes, then we die."
Gabby: "You're old..."

dying beautifully

I love the fall. I was born and raised in Minnesota and now I live in Texas. One of the things I miss most about Minnesota is the change of seasons. I love the weather, the sweaters, and the food. I love how I can gain 5lbs and no one knows because I have to wear layer upon layer of clothes. But the things I think I love the most are the colors that the leaves turn in the fall. They go from green to beautiful yellow, orange, and red. What is interesting about this process is that the leaves are turning these colors because they are dying. I love the green, but the leaves on these trees are the most beautiful...when they are dying.

I think this is a beautiful picture of our lives when they are surrendered to the Lord. We may have done great things before we knew Jesus. Our leaves are green, but after we turn from our old lives, we in essence "die" to our old life and begin a journey of dying to ourselves daily. I know it doesn't sound glamorous, but this produces the most beautiful and vibrant lives. 1 Peter 2:24 (NLT) says, *"He personally carried our sins in his body on the cross so that we can be dead to sin and live for what is right. By his wounds you are healed."* I love the part "live for what is right." There were so many times before I gave my life to the Lord that I thought I was living for what was right. I was living for a paycheck, for recognition, for having a good time, but all of those things left me feeling empty. When I started living for what is right in the sight of God my whole perspective changed.

Every day I choose to die to my selfish desires. Every day I choose to do what is right. Every day I die beautifully. Every day I look less like the world and more like Jesus. When Jesus steps in, our whole mission changes. We go from doing what feels good, to doing what Jesus says is good. And doing what Jesus says is "good" isn't always pretty. Raising our kids, not pretty. Feeding the homeless, not pretty. Holding the hand of a mom who just lost her son to cancer isn't pretty. Bringing food to a friend that overdosed because you know they need a friend and hope, isn't pretty. Allowing your heart to break for the things that break God's isn't pretty. None of these things are "pretty" by the world's standards, but they are BEAUTIFUL by God's standards. *"And the King will say, 'I tell you the truth, when you did it to one of the least of these my brothers and sisters, you were doing it to me!'"* (Matthew 25:40).

We do all these things because we know what true freedom looks like and we know the One who sets us free. We do these things not for recognition, but because by His cross we have been healed. We are healed from addiction. We are healed from fear. We are healed from anger. We are healed from rejection. We are healed from doubt. We are healed from (fill in the blank). We want those around us to experience the freedom we have. That is why we do it, to point them to Jesus.

So, as you go about your day and your life remember how beautifully God sees you. He sees you as you sing that song for the 1,000th time to your child. He sees you crying in a closet because you don't want to take out your frustrations on your child. He sees you as you turn down an invitation to go hang out with your friends so you can watch your child in the school play. He sees YOU as you lay down your selfish desires for HIS desires. You are dying beautifully for a Savior that died for you.

for reflection:

- What things have you had to sacrifice to be a mother?
- Are you resentful about it?
- How has sacrificing been a blessing to you?

"Brayden, why don't you want to take Karate?"
"Because I don't like people telling me what
to do! I just want to break boards and kick stuff."

obedience

Personally, I hate being told what to do. I think that may be where some of my children get this trait. I learned very quickly in boot camp that I had to be okay with being told what to do because it was actually for my benefit. We weren't being told what to do because the division commander had a big ego and just wanted to boss everybody around. It was to train us for when we graduated and would be sent to a ship. Learning to listen and obey commands prepared me for the things I would run into in my future so that I would know what to do when I got there.

This same principal translates to our relationship with God. I didn't want to be told what to do for the longest time. I didn't want to take my problems or concerns to God because I knew His solution wouldn't be what I wanted to hear. Instead, I tried to figure it out on my own. These decisions actually hurt me in the long run. One day it dawned on me: doing it my way was not working...at all. I finally started to take my issues to the Lord and humbly laid them at His feet, asking Him what I needed to do.

Can I be honest? This process was not fun. I had to submit to God's way of doing things, which often wasn't the way I would do them (which I was convinced was the only correct way of doing them). As time went on, I noticed(while challenging at the beginning)the result of my obedience was worth it. Things didn't always turn out the way I would have loved them to, but it is what God wanted, and I had peace about that. It says in Isaiah 55:8-9 (NIV),*"For my thoughts are not your thoughts, neither are your ways my ways,' declares the LORD. 'As the heavens are higher than the earth, so are my ways higher than your ways and my thoughts than your thoughts.'"*

Jordan and I were a part of an amazing church. We were on the leadership team, we loved the pastors, and we never saw ourselves going anywhere else. Until God said, "It's time to go." I remember pleading with the Lord, insisting that He was wrong and we needed to stay. I remember crying until I couldn't cry anymore. I felt devastated. When God told us we needed to go, we had a really difficult time being obedient because we knew we were called to ministry, but God hadn't told us where He wanted us to go next. So we met with our amazing pastors to share the news with them, and the transition to leave began. This was a blind leap for us because we had to trust that God knew what He was doing. His ways are better than our ways, so we had to release control of the situation and let God do what only God can do.

Little did we know God was working behind the scenes moving a beautiful family to Dallas to plant a church. We didn't know they would need leaders to surround them and run with them, to pioneer with them and to dream with them. God planted us in this new church to do just that. We have had the honor to serve and to lead in this world-changing church, and we get to see things happen on Earth as they are in Heaven.

When God said "Go" we didn't understand why, but we were obedient and went. Now we see why. He had a new assignment for us. What would our lives look like if we hadn't obeyed him? What would your life look like if you were obedient to Him in all things? Even the things that don't make sense to us? Trust that when He closes one door He is going to open another one. His plans for your life are good.

for reflection:

- What is God telling you to do?
- What are you afraid of stepping out and doing? *God is not going to tell you to jump and not catch you. Trust Him, his ways are far better than our ways.*

"Mrs. Mauriello? Don't worry, I'm not calling about his behavior today."

the refining process

I got these phone calls pretty often for about a year; my kid was *that* kid in his class. Let's be honest, aren't we all a work in progress?

One morning we decided to stop at an estate sale. I was walking through a gentleman's home (don't you think this is a strange thing we do- walk through someone's house and ask them how much their things cost?), and I saw this beautiful old dresser. I had been looking at them online and there was no way I was paying full price for one. So there it was, covered with old tools, layers of chipped paint and dirt. I made Jordan ask how much it was because he loves to haggle with people. This guy had no idea what it was worth because we walked out of there with it for $35!

We got it home and I already knew where I wanted it to go, but first I had to do a lot of work to re-finish it. There were a lot of intricate details in the wood that the layers of paint had covered up and I wanted to strip it down to the bare wood. This was a bigger undertaking than I anticipated. I feel like those DIY shows and magazines set me up for failure! I would sand an area over and over again, wipe the dust away and see that I hadn't gotten to the wood yet. I had to get a paint stripper and a toothpick to get the paint out of the details in the wood. I had to take off the hardware, let it sit in vinegar, then use steel wool to clean off the years of dirt that had accumulated on it to get it to shine again. Because I wanted to make sure that it was done right, it was a very lengthy process that took attention to detail and a lot of patience.

day twenty-one

About half way through this process God asked, "This is time consuming, isn't it?" and my response was, "YES! Is there some sort of prayer to make this go faster?" He said, "This is what it looks like when I send my children through the refining process." Man, isn't that the truth! Speaking from the position of the dirty painted dresser, being sanded is not pretty or fun, but it is necessary to have the paint and dirt of life removed to bring me back to who God created me to be in the first place.

Often times He will start with fine grain sandpaper, then work His way to a rougher one. Then He gets all up in the intricate details of our life and cleans those out too. He will then take the hardware of our life, like the gifts and talents we have, and clean them off so they can shine. I think taking the time to polish our gifts and talents would be pointless if the "dresser" was a hot mess. This process is ongoing. The refining process is more challenging in some seasons than others, but the process is never-ending until Jesus takes us home. And we need to be ok with that. John 3:30 says, *"He must become greater; I must become less."* That is what this process does to us; it strips away the unholy nature and desires in our heart to transform us to look more like Christ.

These "refinishing" seasons aren't glamorous, but they are necessary for us to become who God has created us to be. I can look back on my life and pinpoint the seasons God has brought me through the refining process. These were the most challenging, but also the most rewarding seasons. There were a lot of tears and moments of frustration, but every time I came out of them stronger, wiser, and ready for what God is going to do with me in the next season. Embrace the refining process. He wants to make you more and more like Christ, to make you a greater witness to the world.

for reflection:

- What season of refining are you in now?
- How are you responding to it?
- Do you become angry or depressed when God sands away the rough edges or when you have to sit in vinegar while God strips away the dirt on your gifts and talents?

"Mom...what's a hater?"

hope

I know I can throw judgments out pretty quickly. I think this can be easy when we don't know all the sides of a story or we don't really know a person.

When Jordan and I went to a leadership conference we were introduced to a very sweet, more mature couple. It was their first time attending this conference as well. We were making small talk about kids and she said her daughter was a fairly well known singer. My immediate thought was, "Aww, that is so sweet she is so supportive of her daughter. I bet I have never heard of her." Then she said her name, and let's just say it rhymes with 'Latey Mary'. In that moment I lost all of my sense and started asking super inappropriate questions about the things I have read or heard on TV. I asked her how she felt about her daughter going from a Christian singer to a secular singer (I must have hit my head really hard that day).Then after I was finished verbally throwing up on this lady I said, "We all go through some mess. I'll be praying for her." Then I walked away. Jordan is always supposed to be my buffer, but even this situation froze him motionless as he watched a train wreck happen before his very eyes. I wish this were a made up story.

This was an insane situation, but I was so quick to judge based off of what I heard on TV or read in a tabloid, even though I don't know her. While I was quick to judge, her mom was quick to speak hope into the situation. Her mom said, "I am believing that she is coming back to God." Her eyes were fixed not on the darkness and hopelessness of the situation but rather on the author and purifier of our faith, Jesus. She wasn't seeing things the way all of us do, which doesn't make her naïve; it makes her strong. She is choosing

day twenty-two

to stand in faith instead of fear. She is choosing hope instead of doubt. This mother recognizes that nothing is too big for God; nothing is impossible for Him. Her daughter has not walked too far for God to save her.

That's what believers do. We recognize when those in our lives are wandering down a destructive path, and we go to Jesus with their cause. In the story of Lazarus (John 11), Lazarus dies and the family puts him in a tomb and seals it shut. He had been in the tomb for 4 days, much too long for anyone to help fix the reality of the situation. He was too far gone for Jesus to do anything, right? We all have those people in our lives who are 'too far gone' who we seal in a tomb and mourn. We talk about their fate, their dark and bleak lives, but we stop going to Jesus about them. Even Jesus can't fix this... can He? We stand before Jesus as he approaches the tomb and say, "but Jesus, he is an abuser." "But Jesus, she has been an addict too long." "But Jesus, he is in prison." "But Jesus, (fill in the blank)." But Jesus shows up to do what only HE can do, bring the dead to life. He stood in front of the tomb that I laid in, without hope and without life, and he yelled, "Raema, come out!" And I rose to life. The life I was meant to live, on the path I was meant to walk, living out the plans and purposes that He created for me to have.

Fortunately, I had people in my life who constantly brought me and my destructive behaviors before Jesus. People who were faithful to pray for me and to believe there was still hope for me. I encourage you today to not give up on people. Do not stop praying for the lost, the hopeless, and the dead. I'm not saying you need to be part of a hurtful relationship, but I am saying that you need to keep praying for them. Even when things look impossible, don't give up on them. What we can often see as a hopeless situation, Jesus sees as an opportunity for a miracle where HE gets all of the glory. Don't stop seeing things with eyes of hope.

for reflection:

- Are there people in your life whom you have given up hope for?
- Are there people that you would say are too far gone?
- How are you talking about these people? With hope or with doubt?
- How can you pray for these people and bring their cause before Jesus?

This is a picture of Asher and Brayden. Aren't they cute?
They were feeding each other dirt here.

"When I grow up I want to be a Jedi"

king of the hill

Our second son Asher and our third son Brayden are only 11 1/2 months apart. They shared a room and would be our "alarm clock" every morning until...Easter. The glorious holiday that celebrates our Savior rising from the dead... unless you are a child. For children it's the day you get so much candy you go into a sugar coma. This day was a turning point for our kids. They finally understood the joy that candy brings, and would do anything at any cost to have candy every hour of every day. The morning after Easter the boys were not our alarm clock. The shock of silence was my alarm clock. I quickly got out of bed because silence from toddlers shoots fear through your bones, and I ran down stairs to find my two boys sitting in a pile of tinfoil- tinfoil that once held Hershey's Kisses. With their faces covered with chocolate, my immediate reaction was, "Well at least I don't have to make them breakfast." Then I wondered, "How in the world did they get those? They were on top of the shelf in the laundry room." Apparently, I have children that learned how to work as a creepy little team at a young age. I saw the kitchen chair pushed up against the dryer, then an empty storage container on top of the dryer. I couldn't even get mad at this point. That was just sheer genius.

I'm not sure at what point in our lives we find it easier to work solo. We can get caught up in trying to 'out mom' the other moms or try to have our families look like a Christmas card 365 days a year, and it's too hard. Did any of you ever play the game King of the Hill growing up? It's a game where you race to the top of a hill and the first one there is the king. But the catch is that there is a group of people that will physically push, body check, or throw you off the hill; so you really have to fight to stay at the top. This is what the life of a mom can

day twenty-three

begin to look like if we aren't careful. It's hard enough for me to stay awake the whole day, let alone try to compete with the other moms around me. What we need is to come together as a team, helping one another to get to the top of the hill instead of trying to pull each other down. This season is hard and we can't do it alone. In fact it would be so much easier if we could do it as a team! Ecclesiastes 4:9-10 (NLT) says, *"9 Two people are better off than one, for they can help each other succeed. 10 If one person falls, the other can reach out and help. But someone who falls alone is in real trouble."*

We honestly aren't supposed be in competition with each other. It isn't healthy. If you are feeling inclined to judge or compete you may want to reflect on why that is. We can feel insecure with the journey that we are on because we might be in different stages than those around us. It makes us question if what we are doing is 'right' or 'good enough.' We don't have to walk through motherhood alone. I need all of you to help me become the mom I need to be to my kids; to learn from you, and for you to help keep me on course. Instead of casting judgment on the mom in the grocery store with the inconsolable toddler who is still wearing her slippers, extend a hand to help her. What if her child is sick and she ran out of food at the most inconvenient time? What if you simply told her she is a good mom? I bet those words would mean the world to her in that moment.

Not sure that you have anything to offer another mom? You may have no experience in that season, but what you can offer is your attention and your time. Sometimes the most valuable thing you can offer someone is your time. When you notice there is a woman in your world that looks like she is drowning, reach out to her. She needs you. She needs your words of encouragement, your smile, your gracious heart, a shoulder to cry on, and a teammate that will cheer her on. I encourage you: if you aren't a part of a group of women that can build you up, create one. You don't need a degree or a fancy title to be the hands and feet of Christ. Don't do life alone.

for reflection:

- Does your church have a women's ministry that you can get plugged into?
- Do you have women in your world that encourage and inspire you?
- Do you know women that need you to encourage them? Invite them over for coffee or for dinner and just invest your time into them.

nobody puts baby in a corner

My senior year of high school I was the captain of our dance team. In the north our dance teams are the equivalent of the cheer teams in the south. We wore a lot of blue eye shadow, had enough gel in our hair that we should have bought stock in it, and we were familiar with the phrase "Kick your FACE." As a senior I obviously wanted to go to the State Championship, so we pushed ourselves hard. At one of the conference competitions in the middle of our performance our music stopped. This had never happened before so we weren't sure what the rules were. Out of panic I screamed, "KEEP GOING!" and we finished the dance while counting the beat out loud. The audience gave us a standing ovation and everyone cheered for us because we didn't quit, even when that was a legitimate response to the situation. I wish I could say we won. We did not, and in fact we had to re-do the performance because it was against the rules to perform without music.

In boot camp I tried to merely be a fly on the wall when out of nowhere I was plucked from my insignificant position to call cadence for the division. In an instant I was placed second in command. Later, I had to fight hard just to get into Search and Rescue School, and it was that much more of a struggle to graduate because I was the only girl in my class, but I did it. I wasn't the fastest or the strongest person in the class but I was nominated by my classmates to receive the "Most Inspirational" Award. During my time in the Navy I received 3 Navy Achievement Medals. Now, I have been in leadership in the church for over 9 years.

I tell these stories not to point to how 'strong' I am or how 'great' I am. I am telling them to show you that we as women can be wired to lead too. Far too often we are led to believe that because we aren't (most of the time) as physically strong as men we aren't capable of leading, or we aren't supposed to lead. Leadership has NOTHING to do with physical strength. It has everything to do with your ability to inspire, to make hard decisions, to encourage, to do things with integrity, and to take things on with boldness and humility. We do not need to sit on the sidelines knowing we are gifted to lead, but simply letting life happen to us. God gave you a voice for a reason. He wants you to use it.

Is leadership easy? NO. But the struggles that come with being in leadership are worth it. And sometimes you will be put in positions to lead where you have no idea what you are doing. I find myself in those places far more often than in places of comfort. 2 Corinthians 12:9-11 says, *"9 But he said to me, 'My grace is sufficient for you, for my power is made perfect in weakness.' Therefore I will boast all the more gladly about my weaknesses, so that Christ's power may rest on me. 10 That is why, for Christ's sake, I delight in weaknesses, in insults, in hardships, in persecutions, in difficulties. For when I am weak, then I am strong."* The longer I am in leadership the more and more I NEED to rely on God to tell me what to do. But I also read about leadership, I watch conferences on YouTube, and I even go to leadership conferences. I do everything I can to learn how to be a well-rounded leader from great leaders.

As I am writing this, I feel someone reading this has been told all her life that she can't lead, or it isn't right that she lead, and she is waiting for permission. Let this serve as your permission. I give you permission to lead. "Nobody puts Baby in a corner!" (*Dirty Dancing* reference). Lead in your job; lead at your kids' school; lead at your church; lead in your community; lead anywhere and everywhere you are passionate. God did not design you to be a doll in a box, set high on a shelf just to be looked at. He has also designed you to lead, and to lead well. He has given you unique abilities that this world needs- that other men and women need. But what if the place where you feel called to lead has only ever been led by a man? You don't need to use manipulation to get anywhere in life, because promotion comes from the Lord (1Peter 5:6). When it's time for you to be there He will get you there. It's our job to be faithful with what we have and where we are leading now.

Go and lead, change the world!

for reflection:

- Where have you been called to lead but have been too afraid?
- Have you believed the lie that because you are a woman you are disqualified to lead?
- Read 1 Peter 5:1-7 in the Message version
- **Extra Credit:** Read *Next Generation Leader* by Andy Stanley
- **Extra Credit:** Read *Climbing the Ladder in Stilettos* by Lynette Lewis

"Hey! Brothers! Try to throw something at my face."

let god be god

"Please God, let me have eyebrows left."

This is the prayer I pray every time I get my eyebrows waxed. And every time I have walked out of the place with eyebrows and my face slippery with baby oil. I know this prayer seems crazy, because I am going into an establishment and asking for someone to wax my eyebrows. Why would I be scared that they would mess it up when this is what they do for a living? They literally rip hair off of people's bodies for a living. (I would love to hear how that conversation goes with their parents. "Mom, Dad...I know what I want to do with my life..."). I go into a room, sit on a bed, and a little lady comes in and pulls hair off of my face. But the fear always rises in me that this time she could mess it up and I'll walk out of there without eyebrows...

This is how we approach God sometimes. When we have something that we need God to fix in us we will go to Him, ask Him to fix it, then worry whether or not He's going to "mess it up." Our conversation with God can sound a little like this: "God, I drink a lot...like, A LOT. I know it has become unhealthy, so please take the desire from me...but please don't ruin my social life because the only place I ever see my friends is at the bar... Amen." That's not how it works. You either give it to God or you don't. There really isn't a gray area.

There was a time in my life when I was so broken, and I had drifted so far from the path that God created for me to walk down that I didn't know if I could ever find my way back. I had tried to fix myself and that only made it worse. I tried to "give it to God" but never really did, so that made things worse. I would never try to wax my own eyebrows- I leave that to the professionals. So why would I try to do God's job for Him? He is the healer of broken hearts, the peace for the weary, and the freedom for the bound.

I clearly couldn't fix me, although I tried. So one day I finally had to say, "God wreck me and mold me back into the woman you created me to be." I had to let God be God and to let Him do His job. Yes, getting Him involved in my problems meant I had to walk away from destructive relationships; not because He wanted to hurt me, but because He wanted to heal me. Yes, that meant I couldn't go to the bar anymore because it would lead to unhealthy behaviors and choices. God wasn't taking anything from me, He was saving me from paths that led to death and destruction in my life. God has never *ruined* anything in my life. He has made my life beautiful. He has removed distractions, dysfunctional behavior, and unhealthy thinking. Not to ruin my life, but because He loves me too much to let me live a life bound to brokenness.

He loves YOU too much to let you live bound to brokenness. I encourage you to let God be God. He has never failed in the past and He isn't going to start now. It may hurt to let go sometimes, but it's so worth it. Just like the pain of getting the hair ripped off my face is worth having two shapely eyebrows...

Here is a prayer for you as you let go:

Father, take (fill in the blank) from me. Be God in this situation. Remove the fear from me as I release this into your hands. I know you want me whole, so God, make me whole. Take the things that are causing me to drift and make me a stronger, wiser, healthier person for it. Help me to see your love for me through this. In Jesus' name, Amen.

for reflection:

- What are some areas that you know you need to surrender to God but you have been afraid He will mess up?
- How do you approach God when you know you need help in letting go of something?

roots

The front of our house was overgrown with climbing vines. It made the house dark and I wasn't sure if there were snakes living in there. Since the snakes here in Texas can kill you, I decided the vines had to be pulled up. I am too cheap to hire someone to do it for me, so I had to make peace with the Lord should I get bitten by a spider or snake and die, and then I started pulling them up. What I thought would be a fast and simple task turned into a painful 3-day project. I would pull up one vine that had a smaller root in the ground, and then realize it was connected to a larger root as well. I wasn't able to just pull it up; I had to use a shovel to dig the larger roots out. I broke all sorts of heavy lifting rules (like lifting with my back instead of my legs), so I walked hunched over like Quasimodo for a couple of days.

While I was pulling up the roots, I began to feel frustrated that it was so hard because of those small vines connected to much larger roots. I just wanted it to be done, but I knew that if I didn't do it right the vines would come back and I'd have to do this all over again. God showed me that this is what it looks like when we begin to allow the Lord to weed things out of our lives that are overgrown and choking out our passion and purpose. A lot of our unhealthy behaviors have a much deeper root, much like the vine being connected to a larger, deeper root. We try to change the behavior, but unless we deal with the deeper root, it will always come back.

I'm not under the belief that everything bad that happens is an attack from Satan. Sometimes when something surfaces like anger, addictive behaviors, lust, or fear, it can be a manifestation of a vine that has a deeper root that has not been dealt with yet. We have to be willing to acknowledge

day twenty-six

that and bring it to the feet of Jesus- let Him deal with it so we can be set free. We owe it to ourselves and to our kids to be set free. I knew that I had to get real with my anger problems that I took out on my husband. I tried to blame it on the devil, but in reality I had a much deeper wound that I never wanted to deal with because I was comfortable with my anger. It was my go-to response and I knew what the outcome would be. Then I saw my marriage falling apart. My kids were scared of me, and this 'attack' had begun affecting those I loved. They deserved better from me. I had to come to a place of humility and admit that I had a problem. It wasn't something I could fix on my own. The only person who could fix it was Jesus. I had to release it into His hands and ask Him to set me set free. He had to go all the way to the root so I didn't have to stay in that dysfunctional cycle.

It says in Galatians 5:1 *"It is for freedom that Christ has set us free. Stand firm, then, and do not let yourselves be burdened again by a yoke of slavery."* I refuse to become a slave to that behavior again because I don't want my kids growing up thinking that behavior is acceptable. I want to break the cycle so my kids don't have to walk down that path like I did.

Now when I stand back and look at my house it doesn't look overgrown and choked out by the vines; it looks clean. This is the same way I felt when the roots were pulled out in my life, and now I can live free. I can breathe and think clearly. This is how God wants all of us to live: completely set free.

for reflection:

- What are some behaviors in your life that keep resurfacing? Pray about whether this is a manifestation of a deeper root.
- Have you allowed Jesus to set you completely free in these areas? This may mean being completely vulnerable with Him and asking Him to go to the root of the problem.

This is me "homeschooling" my boys.

"These mashed potatoes taste like play doh."

power of your testimony

There was a summer that I was absolutely convinced I needed to home school my kids. There was no changing my mind. I purchased an insane amount of curriculum and just dove in. I read all the blogs, looked up all the local co-ops I could join so my kids would be "socialized," and I thought I was ready. I was going to be the best home school mom that has ever graced this planet. I got about 2 weeks in and started to question my levels of sanity. Why on Earth would I think this was a good idea? Why would I start with three kids in three different grade levels? I don't know how to teach people how to read! I can barely read! And math? Um, *no!* I had to take two remedial math classes just to be able to take my mandatory math class for my degree. I was seriously unqualified for this! I enrolled them into school about 6 weeks later, and I'm okay if you call me a quitter. I have so much respect for women who home school their kids. They are my heroes.

Life has yet to turn out the way I expected. I got married when I was 20, and when I was younger I thought I never wanted kids. Now I have four. I wanted to be a chemical engineer and now I'm a pastor. I was raised in Minnesota and now I live on the surface of the sun (aka: Texas). So many things have happened in my life that I never anticipated. I have made so many poor choices and I'm embarrassed I didn't learn things the first time. I have had my heart broken and I have broken hearts. I have lived *a lot* of life in my short 32 years. I could look at my experiences and think I deserve to live with shame and guilt for the rest of my life OR I could look at all of my experiences as testimonies of God's goodness, grace, and mercy.

We all have parts of our life that we aren't thrilled about, that we look back on and wish had never happened, or decisions we wish we hadn't made. Decisions that hurt us or those around us. But all these things can be used as a part of your story to show people how big our God is. I decided that I wasn't going to live under a rock anymore; I wasn't going to live under the heaviness of shame anymore. Instead, I decided to speak up, to be honest about my past and the decisions that I've made, because my honesty and transparency may set another woman free or it might prevent someone from making the same decisions that I made. Revelations 12:11 says, *"They triumphed over him by the blood of the Lamb and by the word of their testimony."* The enemy would love nothing more than to keep us under the impression that the blood that was shed on the cross does not apply to our lives, but it does. I REFUSE to be blackmailed by the enemy with my past. Because the blood applies to all of us, we can use our testimonies- how we were once lost but now found, how we were once bound but now are free, how we were once dead but now are now alive - to bring hope to those around us.

There are people in your life who are going through something you have already walked through, but are too ashamed to say anything because they are filled with so much guilt they don't think you will understand. Our testimonies serve as a beacon of hope. They get to see how Jesus has completely restored us and set us free. We get to share with them the truth that they too can be set free. I don't go around boasting about the sins from my past, but I do boast about how big my God is and how he radically saved me. Romans 5:20-21 (MSG) says, *"But sin didn't, and doesn't, have a chance in competition with the aggressive forgiveness we call grace. When it's sin versus grace, grace wins hands down. All sin can do is threaten us with death, and that's the end of it. Grace, because God is putting everything together again through the Messiah, invites us into life—a life that goes on and on and on, world without end."*

I encourage you to get bold about sharing your testimony. If people judge you, that's their problem. But you never know how far-reaching your testimony will be. There was a woman who came to a conference I spoke at who was there merely as support for a young girl who had come with her. She heard my testimony from that stage and it stuck with her. About three months later she came looking for me because she had recently drifted and needed to know that there was hope for her too. I repeat: you never know who God will set free with your testimony.

for reflection:

- What is your testimony? Write it down.
- Are you afraid to share your testimony? If so, why?
- What have you walked through that could help set someone free or give someone hope for his or her future?

"MOM, God is a magician....right?"

god's lighthouse

When we moved into our new house we faced some interesting situations that we had not faced before. In November we had a massive ice storm… in Texas. All the power went out and it was freezing outside. The power stayed out for over thirty hours and we were iced into our neighborhood. When it got dark we had to rely on candles for light. We needed those candles to see where we were going, what we were eating, for everything! When it got dark we would all huddle around these candles because there was something about being in the dark that felt lonely and cold. When the power finally came back on we couldn't have been more grateful for something we normally took for granted.

When we were all huddled around one candle God said to me, "People need the light that you have like you need the light from this candle." That night He opened my eyes to those in our lives who have been wandering around in the darkness looking for light. I was often easily frustrated by how people who were a hot mess seemed to be drawn to me. I would ask God, "Why do all of the completely lost seek me out?" It's because they are drawn to light. The darkness of the world has left them feeling lonely and cold.

I used to use my kids as an excuse to not engage with the lost and broken people of the world. "So sorry, I can't meet with you because my kid has a cough." Is it technically a lie when my kid did cough, like once? Then I had a light bulb moment and realized people need what you and I have. It's not just our kids who need us, but grown people as well. We can't hide in a closet waiting for the rapture to come because of how dark the world has become. The world is curious about, and is drawn to, the "something different" about all of us who have surrendered our lives to the Lord. Jesus says in

day twenty-eight

John 8:12, *"I am the light of the world. If you follow me, you won't have to walk in darkness, because you will have the light that leads to life."* They are curious about this freedom we have. We have peace in the midst of chaos. We have joy when everything falls apart around us. It's because light illuminates everything around it, and you can see. It can be scary to stumble around in the dark because you aren't sure what is in front of you and what dangers lay before you, but with light everything becomes clear.

These lost and broken see the light of Christ in each of us and they want what we have. Don't be surprised when you end up sitting next to the weepy lady at the park who has lost everything and has hit rock bottom. Don't be alarmed when you are in a room full of women who look like they have it all together, but are drawn to you because they feel empty and hopeless. Stop being frustrated when you get positioned in places where God wants you to shine the light of Christ on the situation. You are a walking lighthouse and He is strategically placing you in dark places to light up His name. In Matthew 5:14-16 Jesus says, *"You are the light of the world. A town built on a hill cannot be hidden. Neither do people light a lamp and put it under a bowl. Instead they put it on its stand, and it gives light to everyone in the house. In the same way, let your light shine before others, that they may see your good deeds and glorify your Father in heaven."* These people are stumbling blindly through life and we have the answers they are looking for. It's Jesus. It's always Jesus. He's the one who can put them on the path of righteousness. He is the one who sets people free. He is the one who saves us all from certain death and destruction, and He may use you in the process.

We are also the example to our children on how to love the unlovable and to show mercy and compassion to those who desperately need it. We teach them how to be the light to those around them. While we may never get a chance to meet all of their classmates or friends, if we teach our kids how to love and extend grace and mercy toward others, they will become a witness to those around them. How awesome would it be if our children bring their friends to Christ because we showed them how?

for reflection:

- Who keeps coming to you for help and direction?
- Have you told them about your testimony and how you were once lost and now found?
- Pray for God to give you the eyes to see those who are stumbling in the dark and need the light that you have.

Brayden: "Dad, do they cut the butts off of chickens before we cook them and eat them?"
Dad: "Nope, that's the best part."
Brayden: "Gross."

you matter
(Guest author: Jordan Mauriello)

Now maybe this isn't the deeper question of life you were really thinking of, but this is our Brayden. Always analyzing, always inspecting, always asking questions (sometimes to the point that it drives you nuts). However, I think the very same thing that drives many of us, the need to have answers, drives him. Maybe at 6 years old his questions are different than yours, but nevertheless, he is seeking answers and that is healthy.

The deeper questions we are really talking about though, are the questions of life that we all seek answers to: "What is my purpose?" "Do I matter?" "Is what I am doing having an impact?" As a husband and father-who would be a completely different person and on a completely different path in life without my wife- I can say definitively...you are making a difference. What you are doing matters. Your purpose is significant and tangible.

I want to take a minute first to talk about the impact my mother had on me. I was always small for my age, and never the most athletic in my younger years. Despite the fact that I loved playing sports (especially soccer), I almost had to play in the age group below mine due to my size and weight difference. This definitely affected my self-confidence, but it never affected my mother's confidence in me. She always believed in me, spoke life into my passions, and took risks on me. When I told my mom I wanted to join the Navy, she was the one who took me to the recruiter while my dad was out of town so I could have my facts all together before I sat down to talk to him about it. I can truly say I would not be where I am today if my mom had not believed in me.

day twenty-nine

Now I am blessed and honored to have a wife who does the same thing for my kids and for me. She is our greatest fan, our strongest supporter, and the reason my kids and I have been as successful as we are today. Proverbs 31:28-29 says *"Her children arise and call her blessed; her husband also, and he praises her:* [29] *Many women do noble things, but you surpass them all."* This is how I think about mothers, a blessing to those they care for.

So let me tell you again: what you are doing matters. It is impactful and could change the lives of those around you. Don't belittle the impact and purpose that motherhood or being a wife has on your family. It is massive, it is significant, and it's one of the greatest gifts you have the opportunity to give to your family.

Believe in your family, your kids, your husband, but most importantly believe in yourself and the great purpose and impact you will have in this life.

for reflection:

- Do you see your role as a mother as significant?
- How do you think what you are doing today will impact the future of your kids?

god's love is better

One night after all of the kids had been put to bed Jordan and I were watching TV. I thought I would spice things up a little and do the "sexy crawl" towards him. You know the one, where the woman is crawling in slow motion and she looks so graceful, and it looks so easy, and where did the fan come from that is blowing her hair? So I thought I would give it a try. As I was crawling one of my legs was on the couch while the other one moved to the ottoman to strategically place myself so Jordan could take in all of my sexy. This wouldn't have been a problem if there had been a rug or something to keep the ottoman in place, but as my life would have it, there was not one. So the ottoman quickly slid away from the couch causing me to fall to the floor trapping me between the couch and the ottoman as Jordan looked over me...laughing. Why don't they show this part of it on TV? I'm suing for false advertisement.

I am thankful that Jordan loves me even when I'm awkward, when I say inappropriate things, when I make stupid jokes, and when I think I'm cool but I am clearly not... not even a little. What blows my mind is that Jordan doesn't love me even close to as much as God does. Often times we see God's love the way that we have seen love displayed here on Earth by those around us. Maybe you perceive love as something that is used as a tool to manipulate. Maybe you see love as something that is used to abuse. Maybe you see love as something to fear. Maybe you see love as something you are unworthy of. Maybe to you love is just an idea or a concept that is truly unattainable.

Love is not something, but love is someone. God is love (1 John 4:8). 1 Corinthians 13:4-8 defines WHO our God is, *"⁴ Love is patient, love is kind. It does not envy, it does not boast, it is not proud. ⁵ It does not dishonor others, it is not self-seeking, it is not easily angered, it keeps no record* of wrongs. *6 Love does not delight in evil but rejoices with the truth. 7 It always protects, always trusts, always hopes, always perseveres. 8 Love never fails.*" Love came down to Earth, clothed in flesh, and love has a face, and love has a name and that name is Jesus. His love for us is not fleeting and it's not temporary. His love extends past our sins and failures. His love is eternal and perfect.

Even when we feel unworthy of His love, His love for us never stops. This rings so true to me because I was once an adulterer. I had drifted so far from God that this behavior had become acceptable to me. I was willing to throw my marriage away, my family away for the desires of my flesh. I had reached my rock bottom and the darkest hour of my life but His love for me still found me in the deepest pit and He pulled me out. While I was still caught up in my sin, Christ died for me (Romans 5:8). By God's infinite grace and mercy He restored my marriage and brought healing to our family. Christ went to the cross so people like me could be restored to Him. Romans 8:38-39 says, "*38 For I am convinced that neither death nor life, neither angels nor demons, neither the present nor the future, nor any powers, 39 neither height nor depth, nor anything else in all creation, will be able to separate us from the love of God that is in Christ Jesus our Lord.*" There is nothing that we have done or will ever do that can separate us from God's love for us.

Maybe you feel completely unworthy of this love. Maybe you are in a place where you feel like you have hit rock bottom and there is no hope for you. I want you to know that He has made a way for you when there was no way. He calls YOU by name. He loves YOU unconditionally. He died on that cross for YOU. With all your imperfections, and with all your sins he died for YOU. There is nothing that you have done that will keep Him from loving you. There is nothing that you have done that will keep that same forgiveness and salvation from you. You have not been disqualified from the love of the Father.

Today ask God to flood your heart with His love. It's unlike anything we will ever experience here on Earth because it's perfect. Open your heart up to His love and let Him teach you how to love those around you.

for reflection:

- How do you receive love from others?
- How has love been abused in your life?
- Have you believed the lie that your past has disqualified you from the love of God?

As I opened a new bag of coffee I said,
"Hey Brayden, you want to know what
Heaven is going to smell like?"
He smelled the coffee, gagged, and said,
"Ew! Heaven smells bad."

Perhaps you picked up this book because of the cover, maybe someone gave it to you, or maybe you heard about it by word of mouth. However you came across this book, I want you to know I prayed for you before this book was ever finished. You are the reason I wrote it. Mothers have a special calling, our capacity is unique, and our work impacts not just our children but generations to come. You are leaving a legacy for your lineage.

Maybe you feel like you have failed in every way as a mother and don't deserve the title. Maybe you had an abortion in the past and now hold kids in your arms, riddled with guilt because of the decision you made. Maybe you are currently or were once addicted to drugs or alcohol, and you had your child taken from your home and you are working hard for sobriety to get your child back. Maybe you suffer from depression, feeling trapped and unable to escape the darkness you find yourself in. Maybe you feel incredibly lonely and isolated. Maybe everything in your life is wonderful. Wherever you are on the spectrum I want you to know that you are not alone. I pray for you daily and I know God has an amazing plan for your life. Hebrews 13:5 says, *"Never will I leave you, never will I forsake you."* That word "forsake" means to leave someone who needs you or is counting on you. Regardless of the things you have done or decisions you have made, God is not going to leave you. God is not in the business of quitting on us, even when we deserve it. He is in the business of giving us chance after chance. Today is a new day, so hit the reset button and start over. Let this serve as your notice to get up, dust yourself off, and start over. We don't get the luxury of quitting; people are counting on us, people are counting on YOU. You can be the mother you always dreamed of being. You can be healed and you can be whole. God is waiting for you to go to Him and place it all at His feet. Nothing is too great for Him.

closing thoughts

I want to close this book with a prayer for you:

Father, thank you for this woman. Thank you for giving her the strength she needs everyday to do what you are calling her to do in this season of her life. Lord, give her peace when her life seems chaotic. Give her the grace she needs to love and to forgive when she feels empty. Surround her with women who will build her up, encourage her, and fan the flame in her life. Thank you for the plans and purposes that you have for her life and the life of her children. Set her focus on you, not the mountains that lay before her. Remove any distractions that stand in the way of her becoming who you have created her to be. I ask that her faith would grow to match your greatness. God, I ask that everything her hands touch would multiply. May she lay her head down at night and sleep peacefully knowing you hold her world in your hands. Protect her and her family from sicknesses and disease. May your hand of blessing rest over her all the days of her life, and may her legacy live on in her children and children's children. In Jesus' name, Amen.

Thank you for dedicating these thirty days to God. My prayer is that you laughed and that seeds were sown in your heart for you to become everything you were created to be. I hope these days brought you closer to the Lord.

love prayer
by Kelsey Askwith

Fill me with your love

Like a spring overflowing

Spilling into life.

Raema Mauriello is a native of Minnesota and currently lives in Fairview, Texas.

She is a graduate of Liberty University with a Bachelor's Degree in Religious Studies and works on the staff at Shoreline Dallas. She also serves as a service pastor alongside her husband Jordan Mauriello.

Jordan and Raema met while serving in the U.S. Navy and have been married since 2003. They have four children: Dominic, Asher, Brayden, and Gabby and a dog who makes running away his job.

Raema is passionate about inspiring people to be who they are created to be and to do what they are created to do. To get weekly inspiration you can follow Jordan and Raema's journey through their blog at www.jordanandraema.com

about the author

Made in the USA
Lexington, KY
17 May 2016